W9-AQH-221

Date: 3/2/16

J 595.728 HAM
Hamilton, Sue L.,
Roaches /

XTREME INSECTS
Roaches

BY S.L. HAMILTON

A&D Xtreme
An imprint of Abdo Publishing | www.abdopublishing.com

Visit us at
www.abdopublishing.com

Published by Abdo Publishing Company, a division of ABDO, PO Box 398166, Minneapolis, MN 55439. Copyright ©2015 by Abdo Consulting Group, Inc. International copyrights reserved in all countries. No part of this book may be reproduced in any form without written permission from the publisher. A&D Xtreme™ is a trademark and logo of Abdo Publishing Company.

Printed in the United States of America, North Mankato, Minnesota.
102014
012015

Editor: John Hamilton
Graphic Design: Sue Hamilton
Cover Design: Sue Hamilton
Cover Photo: National Geographic
Interior Photos: Alamy-pg 7 (inset); AP-pgs 26-27; Corbis-pgs 12-13 & 17 (inset); iStock-pgs 1, 2-3, 4-5, 6-7, 25 (inset), 29, 30-31 & 32; Judith Mulhuijsen-pg 28; National Geographic-pg 9 (inset); Science Source-pgs 8-9, 10-11, 14-15, 16-17, 18-19, 20-21, 22-23 & 24-25.

Special thanks to Martyn Robinson, Naturalist at the Australian Museum.

Websites
To learn more about Xtreme Insects, visit:
booklinks.abdopublishing.com
These links are routinely monitored and updated to provide the most current information available.

Library of Congress Control Number: 2014944885

Cataloging-in-Publication Data

Hamilton, S.L.
  Roaches / S.L. Hamilton.
    p. cm. -- (Xtreme insects)
  ISBN 978-1-62403-691-0 (lib. bdg.)
  Includes index.
  1. Cockroaches--Juvenile literature.   I. Title.
  595.7/28--dc23

                          2014944885

Contents

Roaches. 4

Body Parts 6

Domestic Roaches

  German Cockroach 8

  Brown-Banded Cockroach 10

Peridomestic Roaches

  American Cockroach 12

  Florida Woods Cockroach 14

  Death's Head Cockroach 16

  Green Cockroach. 18

Feral Roaches

  Sun Tiger Cockroach 20

  Rhinoceros Cockroach. 22

  Madagascar Hissing Cockroach. . . 24

Roaches in Medicine 26

Can You Eat Them? 28

Glossary. 30

Index 32

Roaches

There are more than 4,500 species of cockroaches. These insects have been on Earth for about 350 million years. Domestic roaches have evolved so they can only live with humans. Peridomestic roaches live outside or adapt to living in buildings. Feral roaches live outside in tropical conditions.

XTREME FACT – Roaches are incredibly tough. Tests have found that some can live for a month without eating. Others have survived underwater for as long as 30 minutes. Some roaches have lived without air for 45 minutes.

Body Parts

Like all insects, a roach's body has three parts: the head, thorax, and abdomen. Each roach has six legs. Some roach body parts vary depending on the species.

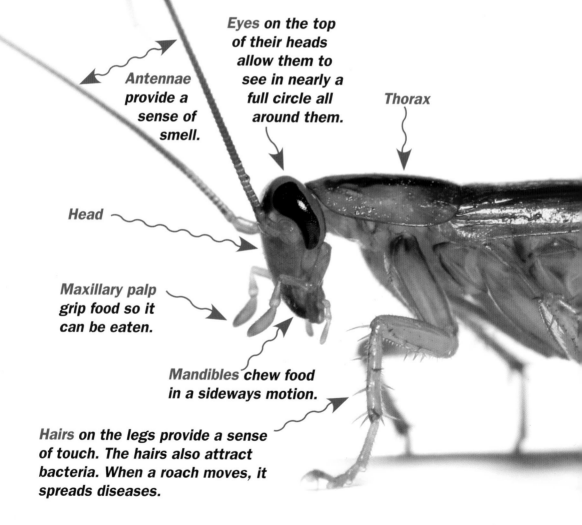

Eyes on the top of their heads allow them to see in nearly a full circle all around them.

Antennae provide a sense of smell.

Thorax

Head

Maxillary palp grip food so it can be eaten.

Mandibles chew food in a sideways motion.

Hairs on the legs provide a sense of touch. The hairs also attract bacteria. When a roach moves, it spreads diseases.

As a cockroach grows, it molts its exoskeleton. A larger one hardens in its place. Depending on the species, this happens 7 to 13 times before it reaches adulthood.

Wings are found on most cockroaches, but not all.

Cercai act as motion detectors, so nothing can sneak up on a roach.

Spiracles are a roach's breathing holes. Roaches do not breathe from their faces, which is one reason why they can live for 9 to 30 days without a head.

Abdomen

Some cockroaches have **claws** or **grippers** on their feet to allow them to move up walls or across ceilings.

7

German Cockroach

German cockroaches are one of several pest roaches that live inside buildings. They are small insects, only about ½ inch (1.3 cm) in length. They move easily through small openings in doors, walls, and floors. They have wings, but prefer to run when there is trouble.

German cockroaches like moist places, which is why they are often found in bathrooms and kitchens. They are omnivores and will eat almost anything. As they move through unclean areas, their legs pick up bacteria. These germs, along with the insects' feces and saliva, are spread throughout homes, often making people sick.

XTREME FACT – German cockroaches are known for their fast reproduction. A German cockroach reaches adulthood in about two months. A female German cockroach may lay up to six egg cases during her lifetime. Each egg case, or "ootheca," contains 30 to 40 eggs.

Brown-Banded Cockroach

Brown-banded cockroaches are a pest species that measure about ½ inch (1.3 cm) long. They prefer warm, dry places. They are known as the "TV cockroach." They live quite comfortably inside of appliances such as televisions or computers. They will eat glue, insulation, and other electronic parts. They also live in furniture, dry cabinets, and ceilings.

Brown-banded roaches are distinctive because of the two bands behind their heads. This is more apparent in young, or nymph stage, insects. Males may fly or jump to escape. Females are flightless.

XTREME FACT– Brown-banded and German cockroaches are unable to live without humans and human environments.

American Cockroach

The American cockroach lives mostly outdoors, but when it decides to live inside buildings, it is a terrible pest.

They are omnivores. They love sweets, but are known to eat anything from pet food to soap, glue, and paint. When well fed, American cockroaches grow to 1.6 inches (4 cm) in length.

XTREME FACT– American cockroaches are not native to America. They arrived on ships from Africa in the 1600s. They have since spread not only all across North America, but all around the world as well.

Florida Woods Cockroach

The Florida woods cockroach is a large, 1.6-inch (4-cm) -long insect. It prefers the outdoor life, but is known to come inside buildings while hiding in firewood.

When alarmed, the woods cockroach may spray a foul-smelling liquid that has given the insect its nickname: the Florida skunk roach. The odorous liquid may squirt out about 3.3 feet (1 m). This helps protect the slow-moving woods cockroach from predators.

XTREME FACT– Many cockroach species, including the Florida woods cockroach, are referred to as "palmetto bugs" because they were first seen living on palmetto trees.

Death's Head Cockroach

The death's head cockroach is native to the forests of Central and South America. It has also migrated to Florida. It is large, reaching up to 3 inches (7.6 cm) in length.

A close-up view of a death's head cockroach's pronotum.

The death's head cockroach is named for the eerie skull-like coloration on its pronotum, above its thorax. Adult death's head cockroaches have wings, but they do not fly. They are flat insects that may squeeze in crevices or under boards to hide.

XTREME FACT– Death's head cockroaches are sometimes used in lab experiments where scientists study such things as their brains, antennae, and movement.

Green Cockroach

Green cockroaches love the warm, humid weather of the southeastern United States, Central and South America, and Mexico. They are also called Cuban cockroaches as they are native to Cuba.

Green cockroaches are good fliers. They grow to about 2 inches (5 cm) in length. They eat fruit, but will also consume many types of vegetation. They prefer to live outside, where they blend in with leaves and shrubs. However, they sometimes enter homes, attracted by fruits or sugary drinks that have been left out.

XTREME FACT– Green cockroaches are also called "banana cockroaches" because they arrived in the United States aboard shipments of bananas.

Sun Tiger Cockroach

The sun tiger cockroach is native to Australia. It is a small cockroach, only .8 inches (2 cm) long. Unlike other roaches, it is active during the day and enjoys the hot sun. Its unique coloration lets it blend in with the dead leaves, fungi, fruit, flowers, and bark it eats on the forest floor.

XTREME FACT– The sun tiger's bright colors and stink glands warn birds, reptiles, and other predators that this insect tastes terrible.

21

Rhinoceros Cockroach

Australia's rhinoceros cockroach is one of the biggest roaches on the planet. It reaches 3.1 inches (8 cm) in length and may weigh up to 1.2 ounces (35 g). It is also known as the giant burrowing cockroach. It uses its shovel-like forelegs to dig a permanent burrow in sandy soil. The nest may go down as far as 3.3 feet (1 m).

Rhinoceros cockroaches like to eat in peace. They drag fallen, dried eucalyptus leaves and tree bark into their burrows. Some food is eaten and some is stored. They help clear forest floors of vegetation.

XTREME FACT– Rhinoceros cockroaches are loners. When two males meet, they fight. They do so by lowering their pronotum and head-butting each other until one runs away or is turned over.

Madagascar Hissing Cockroach

The island of Madagascar, just off the southeastern coast of Africa, is home to this huge insect. It grows to about 3 inches (7.5 cm) in length. It does not have wings, but scavenges for fruit and leaves on the forest floor.

XTREME FACT– The hiss from a Madagascar hissing cockroach comes from the insect expelling air through its spiracles, or air holes, on the sides of its abdomen. The hiss startles predators, and can be as loud as a lawn mower or hair dryer!

Spiracles

Roaches in Medicine

Cockroaches live in some of the dirtiest places: from sewers and garbage dumps to kitchens, bathrooms, and basements. Yet they do not get sick. They are immune to many kinds of powerful bacteria.

XTREME FACT– People in China have been using the American cockroach species for a variety of health benefits for centuries.

Scientists studying why cockroaches remain free of infections have discovered that within a roach's small brain resides chemicals that kill bacteria completely. Tests are being conducted with ground up roach brains to see if these filth-dwelling insects can help humans fight infections and diseases. Instead of making people sick, cockroaches may someday help keep people healthy.

Can You Eat Them?

Certain cockroaches are edible. Roaches are a good source of protein. People in eastern countries such as China, Vietnam, and Thailand eat them fried, toasted, sautéed, or boiled. Edible roaches are raised on fresh fruit and vegetables. Pest and scavenger roaches should NEVER be eaten. They often carry bacteria and disease.

A pan of cockroaches being sold by a food vendor in Thailand.

Glossary

BACTERIA
Single-celled organisms that often cause illness and disease in humans.

BURROW
An underground home.

DOMESTIC
Regarding animals; something that must live with humans to survive.

EXOSKELETON
The hard outer surface that frames a cockroach's body. In order to grow, roaches molt their exoskeleton and a new, larger one hardens in its place.

FECES
Waste matter, poop.

FERAL
A wild creature. Something that does not live with humans.

MANDIBLES
Strong, beak-like mouth organs that are used for grabbing and biting food.

MOLT
Insects shed their outer layer, or molt, in order to grow bigger. Many insects molt several times before reaching adulthood. Some insects eat their molted outer layer.

OMNIVORE
A creature that eats anything–plants or animals.

OOTHECA
A cocoon-like case that holds the eggs of insects such as roaches.

PERIDOMESTIC
A creature that may live in the wild or adapt to living with humans.

PRONOTUM
A plate-like protective covering that rests on top of an insect's thorax.

SPECIES
A group of living things that have similar looks and behaviors, but are not identical. They are often called by a similar name. For example, there are about 4,500 species of cockroaches.

SPIRACLES
Small openings on an insect's body through which it breathes in air.

THORAX
The middle section of an insect's body between the head and the abdomen.

Index

A
abdomen 6, 25
Africa 13, 24
America 13
American cockroach
    12, 13, 26
Australia 20, 22

B
bacteria 6, 9, 26, 27, 28
banana cockroach 19
brown-banded
    cockroach 10, 11

C
Central America 16
China 26, 28
Cuba 18
Cuban cockroach 18

D
death's head cockroach
    16, 17
domestic roaches 4,
    8, 10

E
Earth 4
exoskeleton 7

F
feral roaches 4, 20, 22,
    24
Florida 16
Florida skunk roach 15
Florida woods
    cockroach 14, 15

G
German
    cockroach 8,
    9, 11
giant burrowing
    cockroach 22
Green cockroach 18,
    19

H
head 6

M
Madagascar 24
Madagascar
    hissing
    cockroach
    24, 25
mandibles 6
maxillary palp 6
Mexico 18

N
North America
    13
nymph 11

O
omnivore 9, 13
ootheca 9

P
palmetto bugs 15
peridomestic roaches
    4, 12,14, 16, 18
pronotum 17, 23

R
rhinoceros cockroach
    22, 23

S
South America 16, 18
spiracles 7, 25
stink glands 21
sun tiger cockroach
    20, 21

T
Thailand 28
thorax 6, 17
TV roach 10

U
United
    States
    18, 19

V
Vietnam 28